CHICKEN◯MICS

Chickenomics
First edition, March 2013

written by Mike, Isaac, and Jacob Hansen
illustrated by Pedro Alves

ISBN 978-1482637786

Once upon a time, there was a farm nestled between corn fields and an orchard of fruit trees.

Every day they each laid one egg, and every day the farmer would collect those eggs and give them some food.

Their food was called "scratch", and it didn't taste very exciting. In fact, there wasn't much to be excited about on that farm.

Every day seemed the same as every other day.

One day the hens held a meeting to talk about it.

They complained, "We're so tired of sitting here laying eggs and getting nothing but scratch every day in return".

Peep watched from the rafters of the barn and listened to the hens complain.

Peep had heard their complaints before, but this time he had a great idea. He was so excited, he lost his balance and tumbled into the middle of their groussing.

The older hens all looked down at him.

Mrs. Henderson said, "Oh, its just Peep. He just fell down again. Run along Peep."

"Wait," chirped Peep. "I have an idea that could help us all!"

The hens all laughed and clucked at him.

"What could someone so small have to say to us?"

Peep felt sad and turned to leave, when Granny Red Hen said, "Quit yer cluckin'! Let the youngin' speak."

Timidly, the young chick began to speak. "Every day the farmer comes and takes one egg from each hen and leaves us scratch. Some of you can lay TWO eggs per day if you really try."

"Get to the point. What's this got to do with me?" complained Lays-a-lot. Laying eggs was easy for her, but she only did one because that's all she had to do.

"Instead of just giving our eggs to the farmer, what if we traded them for something other than scratch?" Peep asked.

"What?" said Mrs. Bigbeak. "If we don't give eggs to the farmer, then I'm pretty sure that we'll become **dinner**!"

Dinner looked up – she hated having that name.

Bigbeak was right. The farmer only wanted to get eggs from them.

Before someone could launch into a speech, Peep explained, "I'm not saying that we should give away ALL of our eggs, just the extra".

"Extra? Wouldn't that mean that we would have to lay MORE?" Windy asked. (Windy Airbonnet wasn't the swiftest chicken on the farm).

"Yes, more." Peep said. "Our eggs are valuable to the farmer. That's why he gives us scratch...and doesn't eat us."

"And scratch is valuable to us! We trade things that are valuable to each other!!" exclaimed Windy. (She was starting to catch-up). Some of the hens got excited, but not all of them were.

Granny Red Hen tried to help. She said, "When I was a little red hen, I was tired of scratch. I found some wheat, planted it, harvested it, and made bread. The bread was great, but I didn't have any help, and it took A LOT of work".

"This sounds like a lot of work too", rapped Lay-Z.

"Well, in a way it is," replied Peep, "but if you don't do something different today, you can't really expect anything to be different tomorrow".

Everyone thought about what was said, and everyone got excited for something different. Then everyone tried to do **everything**.

Each chicken tried to lay an extra egg. They all tried to pluck their extra soft feathers.

The next day, the farmer came by. He saw extra eggs and piles of feathers everywhere. He wasn't sure what had made things different, but was happy to take the extra eggs – and leave the same amount of scratch that they got every day.

Peep was as confused as the rest. Then he realized, "Maybe it isn't worth it...to the FARMER!"

Everyone was listening.

"The farmer only expects 12 eggs, so lets only give him 12!" Peep continued before they could get any more confused. "Lets give our extra to **someone else.**"

The chickens loved the idea, but no one loved the idea of doing everything like Red Hen did.

Windy Airbonnet suggested, "Why don't we each do what we do best? If we work together, we can all be happy." (This was a unusually deep insight from Windy).

This got the chickens excited again, and they got to work.

Everyone loved trading. Those that could lay extra eggs laid as many as they could. Moltylocks gathered her extra feathers and made pillows. Peep found friends to trade with.

The dog gave chickens rides around the farm. The cat brought them things that looked like jewelry, and the mice delivered extra fruits from the orchard.

Over the next few months everyone on the farm worked hard and grew happier.

The chickens got more of what they wanted. The farmer got his 12 eggs and continued to give them protection and scratch. The dog got a few eggs every week. The cat got a feather pillow. The mice got fresh straw for their homes.

Peep even found a flock of vegetarian quail who wanted to trade free range worms for their scratch.

Everyone was happy.
Peep was a hero!

...thus we see how one very, very
small and very, very smart chick
who was sick of scratch, made
the whole farm a better place.

For more adventures with Peep, Visit
www.bigideachildrensbooks.com
to see new stories and ideas!

What is Chickenomics?

Chickenomics is the story about choices...and chickens. There are basically seven concepts that form the core principles of Peep's adventure:

1. **Opportunity Cost.** The cost of making a choice is everything you didn't choose. *The chickens' opportunity cost of giving an egg to the farmer was the ability to give that same egg to someone else.*

2. **Specialization and the Division of Labor.** Doing something really well instead of trying to do everything. *As a young chick, Little Red Hen planted, gathered, and baked wheat into bread. It took a lot of work to get what she got. Peep would have suggested sending friends out to do what they do best.*

3. **Exports and Imports.** Things you trade outside of your area. *The chickens never thought of trading eggs with each other because no one would really benefit.*

4. **Incentives.** The thing you expect to happen when you make a choice. *Even though it was more work, the chickens produced more eggs because they expected to get new things. They were also always motivated to produce the minimum because they expected to become dinner if they didn't.*

5. **Scarcity.** The reason why something is valuable. *A weasel that tries to trade dirt for eggs won't do well because dirt is so easy to get.*

6. **Taxes and Transaction Costs.** The cost of doing business. *The chickens wanted to use all their eggs to trade for new things, but they realized that they would always have to give some to the farmer in order to keep getting food and protection.*

7. **Profit and the Invisible Hand.** The natural way that trade makes everyone happier. *Once they decided to work in a different way, the chickens became more comfortable. The more comfortable they were, the happier they were about laying eggs. Also, when one chicken did something new with her feathers, the other chickens would get new ideas. Over time, all their products were better.*